Little Samurai

©2024 by Alfonso A. Matos
All Rights Reserved.

No part of this book may be used or reproduced by any means: graphic, electronic, or mechanical, including photocopying, recording, taping or by any information storage retrieval system without the written permission of the author except in the case of brief quotations embodied in critical articles and reviews. Because of the dynamic nature of the Internet, any web addresses or links contained in this book may have changed since publication and may no longer be valid. Although every precaution has been taken to verify the accuracy of the information contained herein, the author and publisher assume no responsibility for any errors or omissions so that no liability is assumed for damages that may result from the use of information contained within. The views expressed in this work are solely those of the author and do not necessarily reflect the views of the publishe whereby the publisher hereby disclaims any responsibility for them.

No part of this book may be used or reproduced by any means: graphic, electronic, or mechanical, including photocopying, recording, taping or by any information storage retrieval system without the written permission of the author except in the case of brief quotations embodied in critical articles and reviews. Because of the dynamic nature of the Internet, any web addresses or links contained in this book may have changed since publication and may no longer be valid. The views expressed in this work are solely those of the author and do not necessarily reflect the views of the publisher whereby the publisher hereby disclaims any responsibility for them.

Editor | Robbie Grayson III
Cover Designer & Interior Illustrator | Robbie Grayson III
Illustrator | Robbie Grayson III

ISBN | 979-8-8692-9000-7

Published by Traitmarker Books
www.traitmarkerbooks.com
traitmarker@gmail.com

Little Samurai

Alfonso A. Matos

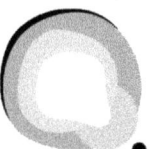

*To God for forging, protecting, and conditioning
my mind to learn from all the good,
bad and indifferent in my life.*

*To my family for always encouraging me
to give my best, regardless of the outcome.*

*To the Dreamers like myself who follow the neverending
pursuit of an idea and boldly turn it into reality.*

*Lastly, to our children who are the future. Though life is hard
and full of uncertainty, continue to drive forward and
let present limitations curb your future.*

*"Your dreams are the preceding paths of greatness
and must be protected at all costs because only
those who dream big can make it big."*

Alfonso A Matos | *Washington DC*

In the heart of a forest, a father, mother, and son were running for their lives. Their footsteps pounded against the earth as the wolves' haunting howls got closer and louder.

Suddenly, the father stopped and turned to confront the angry predators. With a roar, he lunged into the middle of them, buying precious moments for his wife and the son to escape.

The mother's cries echoed through the trees as she sprinted deeper into the forest and up a ravine, her little son right next to her. With trembling hands, they scrambled up the rocky face. Just as they were about to crest the cliff, a wolf's savage grip snatched the mother, leaving the little boy on the cliff alone.

As the wolves made their way up the rock and the shadows of the forest closed in around the little boy, a gigantic samurai appeared out of nowhere. With swift precision, he dispatched the wolves in a matter of minutes.

"Where do you live?" Big Samurai asked the little boy as he helped him up.

"I live in the big town about a day's walk from here." Putting on a brave front, the little boy wiped the tears welling up in his eyes.

Big Samurai looked at the rocky landscape around him.

"Well, good luck." He handed the little boy a little sword. "Be careful," he said, "The sword is sharp, and stay high in the trees as soon as it gets dark. so the wolves can't reach you."

As Big Samurai turned to walk away, the little boy grabbed his arm.

"But can you help me get home?" The little boy tried his best to sound brave. "I have a little brother and grandmother waiting for us." He paused for a moment. "Well, for me."

Big Samurai looked at the boy with a stony face. Then he squinted his eyes.

"Okay. But I'll only take you halfway."

They walked for a few hours until nightfall. It was freezing as they made camp and a fire. Big Samurai gave the little boy his cloak.

"You sleep while I keep watch to make sure the wolves don't come back."

Proudly and trying to be brave, the boy said, "I can stay up. I'm not afraid. And I'm not that cold."

Big Samurai looks over and says, "Look before you act. Follow not those who follow the water current without reason."

"OK. But what about you?" asked the little boy.

"I'll be okay."

As they continued on their way in the morning, they came across a field of flowers filled with sharp lime weeds and buzzing with bees. Big Samurai took off his forearm guards, adjusted them, and gave them to the little boy.

"Here, put these on. You will need them to deflect cuts from your arms and face. As for the bees, you keep running until you get to the other side. Understand?"

"Yes," the little boy said, strapping on the guards.

"What about you?" asked the little boy.

"I'll be okay."

Continuing on their way, they reached a river. Big Samurai took off his shin guards, adjusted them, and gave them to the little boy. He also handed him a pair of sandals.

"Here, put these on. They will protect you from sharp rocks and dangerous fish. As for the current, when you feel it pull you, keep moving to the other side. Understand?"

"Yes," said the little boy, putting them on. But as soon as he waded into the water, he felt a sharp bite, lost his balance, and the current began to pull him under.

Big Samurai dove in, grabbed the little boy, and helped him across.

"Look before you act. Follow not those who follow the water current without reason," Big Samurai said as he set the little boy down.

"I will," said the little boy as he hopped up and down on one foot because of a bite he had gotten on the other. Then the little boy noticed that Big Samurai had been badly bitten several times.

Are you okay?" The little boy asked.

"I'll be okay."

Toward the end of the day, they reached a mountain.

"Here, put this helmet on. It will protect your head from the rocks that can roll down on you and crush you. If you hear a rock slide, get out of its way. Understand?"

"Yes," said the little boy, putting the helmet on.

Suddenly, a large boulder dislodged above them and began rolling toward the little boy. Big Samurai cut the boulder in two with his sword, shattering the rock into a thousand pieces.

One large piece of the rock injured his shoulder.

"Are you okay?" the little boy asked.

"I'll be okay."

After climbing the mountain, they had a clear view of the little boy's village.

"Look, we're almost there! Come on!"

Big Samurai surveyed the landscape around them.

"I have brought you more than half-way. You're almost home. You go ahead on your own. You will be okay without me."

"But we've come this far," the little boy said, disappointed. "I couldn't have done it without you. And for all the help you gave me, you have hurt yourself. Why don't you just stay?"

Big Samurai looked at the little boy thoughtfully, squinting his eyes and grimacing from the injuries he had gotten from taking care of the boy.

He carefully sat down against a rock.

"I gave you my forearm guards to protect your arms from the sharp grass and bees. I gave you my shin guards and sandals to protect your feet and legs from the riverbed and water creatures. And I gave you my helmet to protect your head from the rocks.

But now I give you *my* sword. Protect yourself, your steps, heart, and mind, and you will be okay. Do you remember how to do that?"

The little boy nodded his head.

"Learn to see before you act. Follow not those who follow the water current without reason."

About the Author

ALFONSO A. MATOS has a background in law enforcement, military consulting, and filmmaking. He is an actor, screenwriter, and executive producer known for his work on various film and television projects, including reception of the IndieFEST Film Award Recipient Nomination. Born in the Dominican Republic, Alfonso developed a passion for storytelling and filmmaking at a young age. Later, he pursued his interest in law enforcement, where he gained extensive experience in gang investigations, intervention, and military consultation, eventually becoming a renowned expert in gang and military affairs.

Alfonso is based in Washington DC, where he enjoys exploring cultural and historic landmarks, spends time with his family, and continues to write screenplays that explore the human experience. Alfonso is set to build on his success as an actor, screenwriter, and executive producer as a fresh face in the action genre. He lives by the motto, "The world is our stage. Perform!"

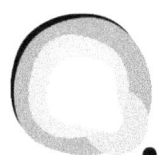

www.ingramcontent.com/pod-product-compliance
Lightning Source LLC
LaVergne TN
LVHW072123060526
838201LV00068B/4963